GOD OF THE JOURNEY

Dare To Have An Authentic Walk With God

Dionne N. Moore

GOD OF THE JOURNEY. Copyright © 2023. Dionne N. Moore. All Rights Reserved.

Printed in the United States of America.

No portion of this book may be reproduced, stored in a retrieval system, or transmitted in any form or by any means, except for brief quotations in printed reviews, without the prior written permission of DayeLight Publishers or Dionne N. Moore.

DAYELight
PUBLISHERS

ISBN: 978-1-958443-25-5 (paperback)

All scripture text used in this book comes directly from the Holy Bible, King's James Version by Thomas Nelson 1798.

DEDICATION

This work is dedicated to every person who desires to fully embrace a genuinely unconventional walk with Christ. Whether you are a new believer or have been saved for years and your relationship has become stale, the Lord desires you to come to HIM afresh, be real with Him, and dare to trust Him to take you on the journey He has pre-destined for you.

It is my prayer that you will allow the Lord to be your life partner and friend and experience the joy of living a uniquely authentic life in Him.

TABLE OF CONTENTS

Dedication iii
Acknowledgments 7
Introduction 9
Section One: The Journey 13
    Seeking One Lost Sheep 14
    Prayer Equals Oxygen 21
    Knowing Who You Are And Whose You Are 28
    Interacting With the Holy Spirit 39
    Opening Of My Spiritual Eyes 39
    Baptism of FIRE 44
    Relationship And Religion 54
Section 2: The Battle Series 59
    The First Tool 61
    The Second Tool 66
    The Third Tool 70
    The Fourth Tool 73
    Prayer as a Weapon 75
Conclusion 81

Psalm of Praise 83

Prayers 85

    Prayer to Receive Salvation 86

    Prayer to Recommit to Christ 87

    Prayer For My Readers 89

About the Author 91

ACKNOWLEDGMENTS

I thank, praise, and give all glory to the precious Holy Spirit who began writing this book and led the process; Your patience with me has been humbling. Thank You for Your counsel, love, leading, and choosing to use this vessel to bring understanding to Your people. You have—true to Your Word—taught me all I need to know thus far, and I trust You to continue and complete this process. You are my Teacher, Friend, Father, and Counsellor. I truly glorify You for sharing Yourself with me.

Special mention must be made of my husband, Nigel Moore Jr., who has supported and encouraged me, and witnessed and embraced the ebb and flow of my growth. I thank God He chose you for me, and I will always love and pray for you.

To Mrs. Yvette Mahoney, who laid the foundation for my faith; Mom, I praise the Lord for the example you set for me, getting me up at 2 am to pray as a teenager and saturating my spirit with worship of our King. Thank you for every prayer you prayed for me that has now become my heritage.

To Ms. Marsha Williams, I am grateful for your loyalty to your Saviour, who uses you for mighty exploits. The prayer warrior you are continues to raise the bar for me; you have demonstrated that prayer is a mighty weapon. You have been a critical part of my family and my walk with Christ; thank you for your obedience to our Lord.

INTRODUCTION

The Word of God says before the beginning of time; *HE WAS* before we were formed; *HE KNEW US,* and at the end of time, we will stand *BEFORE HIM.*

Have these questions ever crossed your mind: "Why am I here? What is my purpose?"

People have asked these two questions for generations over; some discover the answer, and some never do. If you are holding this book in your hands, then you too have asked yourself and may have prayed, cried, or even demanded GOD to reveal this mystery to you. The funny thing is, the answer is very simple, and I will tell it to you now rather than at the end of this book.

YOU are here because GOD, the Father, wants to have a *RELATIONSHIP WITH YOU.* Your purpose is to display or reflect His GLORY so that it draws others to HIM. Point blank! His desire is to be present in your daily life, sharing in what you go through, and, ultimately, have you live as a citizen of HIS Kingdom to affect the world around you.

God of the Journey

This book was spontaneously inspired by the Holy Spirit. I love to write, and as I began my walk with Christ, I began to write everything down, finding everything about Christ intoxicating, scary, and confusing all wrapped in one bundle. In an effort to transfer all I had written to digital to preserve the information, I sat with my tablet one afternoon at work, and as soon as my fingers touched the keyboard, these words began to pour effortlessly from me. As time elapsed, the Holy Spirit would give me another section to do, and then another. He has intimately led this whole process and has chosen what He desires to be a part of this book.

There are three general sections to delve into; section one intertwines my life experiences and lessons with how the Word of God positions itself in that moment, covering how God called me to Himself, learning the similarity between prayer and oxygen, and understanding who and WHOSE I am. Intimate interactions with the Holy Spirit are detailed in this portion, including how my spiritual eyes were opened and my unusual baptism.

The second portion of this book walks you through the 'battle series' – as the Holy Spirit calls it. This is where I relay verbatim what the Holy Spirit has taught me are the most important tools for battle. These lessons were shared in the still of the early mornings during my devotions with Him.

Finally, in the third section, we do what pleases Him; lift a psalm of praise and spend a few moments together in prayer.

The intent is to continue, along with other children of God, to solidify, through my experiences, that the desire of the Father is for people to understand what it means to practically and authentically walk with Him and live as Kingdom citizens.

Through this book, I invite you to share the first year—my real first year—with JESUS. My prayer is that it will stir you to think deeply about having a truly authentic relationship with HIM who desires you, rather than following basic religion, that you will become intimate in knowing Him as your Creator, Saviour, and Judge. My hope is that my journey will show you that life will present challenges that must be navigated through a RELATIONSHIP with JESUS, which is a process just like anything else in life. However, like I did, maybe you will see that we make it harder than it really is, so take a deep breath and let's go.

SECTION ONE:

THE JOURNEY

Seeking One Lost Sheep

How think ye? If a man have an hundred sheep, and one of them be gone astray, doth he not leave the ninety-nine and goeth into the mountains, and seeketh that which is gone astray? (Matthew 18:12 – KJV).

The life you choose to live is never the one you are truly designed to live, and I never understood this until the LORD of heaven decided that it was now or never.

I grew up mostly under the Baptist umbrella of religion, and at the age of twelve, I was water baptized and was going to church almost daily. My mother, being all consumed with Christ, made sure we; my brother, sister and I were present before the church doors opened, participated in everything, and were the last set of persons to leave after the church was locked. She worked hard at instilling the Word of GOD in my little head.

Train up a child in the way he should go, and when he is old, he will not depart from it. (Proverbs 22:6 - KJV).

I was doing okay until puberty hit, then things became, shall we say, *murky*. As time went on and years passed, I drifted farther away from the LORD and began to do my own thing. We have all been there, and some of us still are. It is a process, trust me.

At the age of forty-one, with husband and son in tow, I was living according to my own rules and thought I was doing well for myself and was happy to know that work provided a valid excuse not to attend boring church, and I never paid much attention to my spiritual life, but the Father had different plans for me and began to put them into action.

Choose you this day whom you will serve. (Joshua 24:15 - KJV).

One day in December 2018, my mother-in-law called me. She sounded quite concerned. "Ms. Dee, I had a dream about you last night. I dreamt that you met in a car accident and you died." For some strange reason, this did not jolt or move me in the least, considering that I almost died tragically at the age of nineteen in a serious motor vehicle accident.

"Really," I responded, "Wow, so what are we doing for the holidays?" I continued, and we chatted away and made our plans.

I have learnt that the God of heaven is quite tactical and uses what He deems necessary to get your attention. Later that same week, my assistant, Marsha, came to me, "Ms. Moore, you know I had a dream that you crashed into a light pole and died. I saw your soul leave your body!" Did it occur to me that I was getting the same message twice in the same week? NOPE!

"Hey, my mother-in-law had a similar dream since week. Go figure." My life was just the way I liked it, filthy and self-serving, blissful in my mind, really. Why would these two dreams stand out to me?

They know not, neither will they understand; they walk on in darkness. (Psalms 82:5 - KJV).

We made plans for the holidays. Marsha went on vacation. We joined our family out of town and had a ball. Then I began to zero in on the most important day in the year: my birthday. You must understand the trauma of growing up in a world where your birthday comes after Christmas, especially living in the Caribbean. "You only getting one present enuh, so choose if is your birthday or christmas present" was the customary statement. Well, now that I was my own woman and a wife, I decided that my birthday was a week-long holiday and schooled my husband and son accordingly. That year we decided to visit Portland and relax.

Just as we were getting ready to leave, I began to smell a very strong odor of gas. This was most concerning. I made a dramatic effort to find out where it was coming from. I asked my husband to check the gas line and examine the gas tank, but *NO ONE ELSE WAS SMELLING THE GAS*. "*I must be losing it,"* I thought to myself. "Well, if there isn't a leak and the burners are off, let's go then," and off we went and celebrated the birthday and new year with our close friends in Portland.

As soon as January rolled in and we returned home, Marsha approached me quite cautiously and said she had a word from the LORD for me. My first thought was, "Wow, I've heard this happen to lots of people. Now it's my turn." I was curious, to say the least. "Please, go ahead," I said.

"I am not pleased with your life; you have spent many of your years focused on yourself." I could hear the nervousness in her voice. *"I have watched you year after year place priority on your birthday, yet never thought to share it with me. I have tried getting your attention. Why do you think you were the only one smelling gas? You neither see nor hear Me. You should have died on your birthday, but I have decided to give you another chance. I love you and desire so much more for you. You have not given thought to your soul. Now I send My servant to tell you, you have one last chance. I have designed a different life for you, so choose now whether you will live for yourself or live for ME."* Marsha impressed how difficult it was to carry and deliver this word, but her loyalty was to her Saviour, and she had to be obedient to His leading.

Well, that was never how I imagined that moment would be, but instantly I became very aware of the dreams, the life I was living, and my own mortality. I thanked her and said it was much to consider. Even though she spoke, I heard **HIM** quite clearly, and my heart testified to HIS truth. I walked into my backyard looking into my life. As my thoughts turned to Christianity, I began to recall how utterly bored I was in the Baptist church, and for the first time in a long time I began to talk to the LORD:

"Lord, I know that Jesus died on the cross for my sins, and You know mine are bad, like really, really bad, and here You are giving me another chance, one I don't even deserve. Thank You for this moment and, yes Lord, I choose to live for You, **but…**" Who comes to salvation on a conditional basis? Yep! Me. "Lord, I don't want that type of boring life that I grew up in. If I am going to live for You, please let it be radical. I want to know without a doubt that You are with me, okay? Radically radical is what I need. Amen."

We have a saying in Jamaica, "Be careful wha you wish fa, cause you juss might get it." I found that the truth to this adage is in scripture:

Therefore I say unto you, what things soever you desire, when you pray, believe that you receive them, and you shall have them. (Mark 11:24 - KJV).

God has honoured this seemingly weird prayer that I prayed.

Dionne N. Moore

I encourage every new believer and persons who think your walk with the Lord has become mechanical to step out and be bold, be yourself with the LORD; He seems to like it!

So here I am, standing in my backyard, just finished my own weird salvation prayer, and then a sentence was just imprinted in my mind: **"At the moment of salvation, all rights and authority of HIS Kingdom become effective."**

At that moment I had no idea what that meant or why it came to me, but it stayed with me. Later that night, as I lay in bed, my mind was racing with both anticipation as well as deep regret. I just opened my mouth and began speaking, "Jesus, how can You even love me though? Look at the life I've been living, it dirty enuh." I shook my head in disgust. "I can't imagine how You sat and watched me all those years do all the terrible stuff I did. Lord Jesus, what do I do now? Do I start calling people to apologize for stuff I've said? How do I reverse any damage I might have done? Do I begin to confess stuff I've done? What...?" As I pondered and spoke quietly to Him, He responded. I heard a still, small voice down inside of me say, **"GO and sin no more."** I shot up in bed. "Was that You, Jesus?" I had heard that somewhere before; it is in the Bible somewhere. I jumped out of bed at 10:15 pm, ran to get the Bible I hadn't taken up in ages, and grabbed google to find the scripture.

When *Jesus had lifted up himself, and saw none but the woman, he said unto her, woman, where are those, thine accusers? Hath no man condemned thee? She said, no man LORD. And Jesus said unto her, neither do I condemn thee: Go, and sin no more. (John 8:10-11 - KJV).*

My fingers could not turn the pages fast enough. I read through the whole story, looked up and smiled and said, "Okay, LORD, I see what You did there." I was overcome with joy! Jesus, the one who died on the cross, the one in the Bible, just spoke to me and the Bible confirmed it. He had singlehandedly, in one day, captivated my attention, shifted it away from self, and blown me away with His mercy. LOVE filled me. I fell asleep with the biggest smile on my face.

Prayer Equals Oxygen

Come now, and let us reason together... (Isaiah 1:18a - KJV).

What an invitation to receive from the eternal, uncreated God of the universe. In our busy lives we often forget that the Father is waiting for us to come talk to HIM. We forget that He gave His Son to die on calvary's cross so that we can be reinstated as His sons and daughters. Do you remember that immediately after Christ died, there was a great earthquake and the veil in the temple was torn from top to bottom? It was for this purpose; to allow us access to come and reason with HIM.

When I just re-committed my life to Christ in 2019, I would get up at odd hours of the morning to pray. I only prayed for maybe ten minutes because I really didn't have anything to say. I would ask the Lord to help me to know what to say, and instinctively I would just wait for another ten minutes and then go back to bed. Why I did that, I do not know. One night as I got up to go back to bed, I heard His still, small voice say, **"Tarry with Me,"** and like an infatuated teenager, my mind instantly went "Wow, He wants me to stay!" So, I sat down and simply said "Yes LORD, I'll stay." I sat there for maybe another half an hour in silent anticipation, and inevitably I fell into a short nap right there. When I awoke, I simply said "LORD, I'm really tired. I'm going to bed. Goodnight."

In the following months, I realized that that act of obedience opened the door for repeated 'date nights.' I would tell Jesus what time I would meet Him, and as I did night after night, He began to speak more often. There were a few nights that I came, sang a few worship songs, and then humbly said "Lord, I'm here to listen to You tonight. What's on Your mind?" Then I would be silent and wait. It would not take very long before the Holy Spirit was sharing what was on the Father's heart.

I am sure many of you are thinking not everybody can hear Jesus speak; not everybody experiences this. I contradict this school of thought because God's Word makes us understand that when you accept salvation through Jesus, the Holy Spirit comes to live within you.

Let us pause to look at the story of the interaction between Jesus and Nicodemus found in John 3. Nicodemus, a learned and important man in his country, came to Jesus in secret to talk with Him. Jesus explained to him that in order to see the Kingdom of GOD, you must be born again. Of course, Nicodemus did not understand, but Jesus' explanation recorded in verses 5-6 proves that the Holy Spirit comes within you upon conversion.

Dionne N. Moore

And Jesus answered, Verily, Verily I say unto thee. Except a man be born of water and of the Spirit, He cannot enter the Kingdom of God. That which is born of the flesh is flesh, and that which is born of the Spirit is spirit.

The Holy Spirit comes to do the "birthing" on the inside of you. That is where He dwells. Remember, our bodies are His temple. Now if the Holy Spirit is inside you, He will speak to you. It is possible to hear the voice of God; the problem is, at conversion, we don't know what to listen for or what to expect; sometimes we try too hard. I remember when I began to have these experiences, I was so excited that I shared it with my mother-in-law. Her response to me was quite sobering, "Ms. Dee, careful of those voices you hearing enuh." Initially, I was crushed. I thought she would have been happy for me, but little did I understand the benefit of her wisdom. Her statement got me thinking and wondering how I could know for sure that this really is the LORD speaking to me. Doubt began to creep in. I called my mother and asked her "How can I be sure, sure, sure that I am really hearing from God?" She shared with me that GOD ONLY SPEAKS THROUGH HIS WORD. Whatever I hear Him say, I must be able to find it in the Bible.

This sent me on a biblical treasure hunt. By this time, I was hearing Him speak quite often. I assembled every piece of paper I had written with what He said and began to look for words or phrases in the Bible. True to life, there they were: HIS WORD. I found that if you begin to acknowledge

God of the Journey

the Holy Spirit as the person He is, and be patient, He will respond to you, and the proof is in His Word.

I began to devour the Word by listening to sermons. This initiated my baby steps process to begin reading the Bible. I was hungry, could not get enough. The more I sponged up the Word, the more Jesus was present. I remember stealing away many days in those first few months during my lunch hour just to be with Him, to talk to Him, even though I did most of the talking. I was anticipating His every word like a lovesick puppy. He was always there, speaking through His Word, bringing a song to mind or saying two or three words in my spirit. That was how we shared many conversations, and we enjoyed each other's company.

There are many excuses that circulate when the topic of prayer arises, chief being "But I don't know how to pray." Prayer has been elevated to a level where we are cultured to think it is hard and everyone else can pray better than we can. Whatever the scenario, I hope what I am going to share will help to shift your view.

PRAYER is simply talking from your heart to God. I explained it to my husband this way: "Every day you normally speak to your parents three or four times at least. You talk to them because you desire to check up on them, to see if they need anything, to share something that happened at work, about our son or the house, and you may share a story and a laugh or two." It is the same thing you should be doing with GOD; the difference is, because the LORD is WHO He is, communication with Him is called prayer.

I know it is easier to talk to people because you can receive an instant physical response; however, you can develop your spiritual hearing by being patient in prayer. Many days, as I said previously, I was chatting away and was always expectant to receive a response. Sometimes I did, sometimes I didn't. When you become a little more intentional in your commitment to Jesus and take time to listen, soon you will begin to understand how He chooses to speak to you.

We hear all the time that prayer is a dialogue, not a monologue. This is true! You must give your partner, the Holy Spirit, an opportunity to respond. Sometimes all I got was a scripture, but when I opened His Word, it came to life in my heart. In your walk, do not put the LORD in a box. Open yourself to speak, but more so, open yourself to listen.

PRAYER is oxygen to your spiritual life. Without it, your spirit man will die. It is the process of breathing that gives life to your spirit. Look at it like this, 'inhaling' is listening to the Spirit of GOD, and 'exhaling' is you speaking to the Spirit of GOD. The beauty of this is, every time you inhale, it fills you with what you need to live and grow spiritually. When you exhale, you cast your troubles upon Him and He helps you through them. Isn't GOD amazing! This is a prime example of understanding how the Holy Spirit uses the natural to make plain something spiritual. He is a wonder, and a mighty GOD.

When you give importance to prayer, actively talking to God, He will show you things and reveal mysteries to you, and it will blow your mind, literally. For many years, I suffered with severe pain in my arms; it was unpredictable. I would be fine for months, and then it just flared up, incapacitating me instantly. It was so bad sometimes that I felt as though I could not catch my breath, and it would run up and down my arm like a train on rails. I never knew what triggered it, which arm it would affect, when it would start or how long it would last. I spoke to numerous doctors and none of them could identify the cause. I came across a pastor, however, who taught me that I could go into prayer and ask the Lord to reveal the origin and solution to problems or challenges that I was facing, so I decided to try it.

I sat down on my couch one early morning and began to simply ask the Lord to reveal the origin of the pain in my arm. I repeated that prayer point for about fifteen or so minutes and decided to wait twenty minutes and then pray it again. As I waited, the Holy Spirit came with the word **"INOCULATED."**

I was so surprised I literally said, "What now?" He continued, **"When you were inoculated as a child in high school, the needle touched and damaged your nerve."** Immediately I remembered the day He was referring to, and I sat there speechless. There was no doctor who could have diagnosed this because I could not even identify where the pain was originating from. I did not think that "Thank You, Lord" was sufficient. All I could say was "Father, I am in awe of You." Then I remembered the other part of the prayer, so I began: "Lord, what is the solution to this issue, because I really can't manage this pain?" It was weeks before He gave me the answer. He, in fact, healed it, but that was a faith walk that I had to walk out.

Prayer is communication; the oxygen of your spirit. Never neglect it. Rather, take time to build your prayer life, get help from persons around you who are strong in this area, and you will find a dimension in Christ that will fuel your growth.

Knowing Who You Are And Whose You Are

For as many as received HIM, to them gave He the power (right) to become the sons of God, even to them that believe on His name. (John 1:12 – KJV).

We often hear that everything in the physical world originated from the spiritual world. I pray, by the grace of God, that I will be able to help you understand how the spiritual realm can be understood through the physical.

Let's take this from a general perspective. When a baby is born, it does not understand anything around it. Regardless, this child has biological parents, who will give this baby all it needs to grow and develop. The child, upon birth, becomes a member of a family, a citizen of a country and, in some cases, heir to whatever its parents own. Now begin to look at this in the same way from a spiritual platform.

There is first the moment you decide to accept Christ as your personal Saviour. You may wonder what happens spiritually at that moment:

That if thou shalt confess with thy mouth the Lord Jesus, and shalt believe in thine heart that God hath raised him from the dead, thou shalt be saved. (Romans 10:9 - KJV).

When you confess with your mouth and believe in your heart that Jesus paid the atonement for your sins, and you decide to accept Him as your Saviour, the blood of Jesus blots out your sins, meaning, His blood becomes the currency that pays the price for your sins. This is what takes you from eternal damnation into eternal life, and then your name is written in the Lamb's book of Life. You are, through this process, *born again.* The Holy Spirit, who raised Christ up from the dead (see Romans 8:11), comes immediately to live on the inside of you, becoming your Teacher and Guide. Jesus becomes your big brother, and the uncreated God of the universe is now your legal Father. Let that sink in for a minute.

Understand that the Creator of all, who needs nothing, has chosen to make us His sons and daughters and dwell within us. This alone is the best gift ever, but it goes deeper because you are now His legitimate child. You are now a citizen of the Kingdom of Heaven, and your birth certificate is found in His Word (see John 1:12). You are now born with all the rights and authorities of His Kingdom as your birthright. Similar to how you grow and learn who you are and how to operate in the natural, the same applies in the spirit. The Holy Spirit is our Teacher and Guide, to help us learn to eat, creep, stand, walk, speak, and then understand the spiritual environment in which we exist. It is not complicated when you look at it from this perspective. Remember, it takes time; it is a process.

Okay, so we know that we are born again. What now? What are these rights we have?

Again, let's use what we know and understand as props so the Holy Spirit can explain, through His Word. Globally, we are born with fundamental human rights that we are led to believe originated in some office years ago by some president or person looking to govern a nation of people. Let's see if we find anything in scripture.

Right to Freedom of speech: Hebrews 4:16, "Let us therefore come boldly unto the throne of grace, that we may obtain mercy, and find grace to help in our time of need." (KJV).

In reverence, through prayer, we can approach our Father with boldness. We can talk to Him, and He will listen. The Lord allows us the freedom to come right in and speak to Him. He is your Father, and this allows you to speak freely, share your thoughts, the things that make you laugh, how tired you are, bills that need to be paid, things that pain your soul; nothing is too simple or too complicated for Him. Believe me, He is interested in laughing with you, crying with you, encouraging you, helping you; all you need to do is speak to Him.

<u>Right to Life: John 3:16,</u> "For God so loved the world that he gave his only begotten son, that whosoever believeth in him, shall not perish, but have everlasting life." (KJV).

Being born again allows you to enjoy the surety that when your physical eyes close in death, this right is immediately activated and you enter eternal joy. Scripture states in Luke 16:22 that angels of the Lord came to take Lazarus to glory. You and I will certainly have the same experience. Our goal is not the grave but the glory of GOD.

<u>Right to Liberty: John 8:36, 2 Corinthians 3:17,</u> "If the Son therefore shall make you free, ye shall be free indeed." (KJV). "Now the Lord is that Spirit: and where the Spirit of the Lord is, there is liberty." (KJV).

Jesus paid the price for your ransom on the cross with His blood, then the Holy Spirit came to dwell in you. How much more freedom do you need?

What believers miss is that we have a right to freedom. The enemy knows that He lost you, but he does everything in his power to deceive you and have you thinking that you failed once and you will always fail. He seeks to trick you into believing you will never get this walk right. The thing is, we are quick to believe the lies of the enemy and sink into self-condemnation rather than believe the words of life that are our right. Romans 8:1 says, *"There is therefore* **NOW NO CONDEMNATION** *to them which are in Christ Jesus,* *who walk not after the flesh, but after the Spirit." (KJV – emphasis mine).*

It is up to us to walk boldly in the freedom that Christ has secured for us with His precious blood. Go ahead and read Galatians 5:1.

<u>Right to Personal Security:</u> *Psalms 91:11-12,* *"For he shall give his angels charge over thee, to keep thee in all thy ways. They shall bear thee up in their hands, lest thou dash thy foot against a stone." (KJV).*

This is a guaranteed provision for children of God who choose to live at the feet of Jesus. Look back at your life and try to remember if you narrowly escaped a serious accident or a plot or scheme someone intended to use to destroy you. These are examples of His love for you, reaching out and pulling you out of harm's way, protecting you and keeping you safe. Our Father is a mighty warrior. David says, "Mighty in battle." (see Psalm 24:8). He knows how to protect you, redirect you and keep you from harm.

We have rights to <u>Education</u> (see John 14:26), <u>Heavenly Healthcare</u> (see Jeremiah 30:17), and <u>Provision</u> (see Matthew 6:25-33). This is just a sample of the promises that God has given to us that we may thrive both spiritually and physically. Take some time to read these scriptures and allow the Holy Spirit to renew your mind.

Dionne N. Moore

What authority do we have?

I hasten to say that we of ourselves bear no authority or power. We are Kingdom representatives and conduits of God's power, but He does not allow babies to play with electricity. Haha, see what I did there. Psalms 62:11 states, *"God hath spoken once, twice have I heard this; that power belongeth unto God."* (KJV).

So, you must grow, mature, and become trustworthy before God allows you to access His power. The fact that it became effective when you are born again, does not mean it is instant. No, we must grow in some things. That being said: We have first and foremost authority over the earth as recorded in Genesis 1:26 and 28. We have the power to heal the sick according to Matthew 10:1. We have the authority to preach and teach God's Word (see Acts 1:8 and 1 Corinthians 1:18). We have authority over devils, to bind and loose (see Matthew 16:19). These are scriptures that you must study. The Holy Spirit will give you understanding.

All this we have gained only through Christ. All of creation, every circumstance, will bow to the Christ in you, for as His own, we take on the nature of Christ and in doing so we stop living according to the flesh (see Romans 13:14). Romans 6:14, which is one of my go-to verses for strength, says this: *"For sin shall not have dominion over you; for ye are not under the law, but under grace."* (KJV). This is a birthright!

God of the Journey

Once you begin to read the Word and allow it to become your GPS, you begin to truly understand who you are and whose you are, and this transforms how you live and operate.

Let's examine how Jesus operated while He lived on earth. Jesus was well-learned in scripture. He was compassionate, loving, and forgiving. He spent many hours in prayer, constantly talking with our Father. He walked in authority, yet He remained humble. He was a no-nonsense kind of guy; blunt when He needed to be, a rebel of sorts. His doctrine was unlike what people were accustomed to and caused many of His followers to either question His message, leave His following, or completely immerse themselves in the truth of Who He is. He never forced anyone to believe; He shared Himself through His message unconditionally.

The Bible teaches that He is the same yesterday, today, and forever (see Hebrews 13:8), that what He has spoken is forever established in the Heavens (see Psalm 119:89), so salvation and all its rights never change because He is salvation. Once you are His, you can be confident that He will stand by His Word.

I am not in any way suggesting that once you are saved, you are always saved. His Word also says the wages of sin is death (see Romans 6:23). If you begin again to lead a sin-filled life, you have separated yourself from Him, and unless you repent—turn back to Him—your portion in eternity will be damnation. That, however, is not His will for you. He has made available to us through His grace a life that is unique and eternal as His sons and daughters.

Let's look at things through the Father's eyes for a moment. In Jeremiah, He says *"Before I formed thee in the belly I knew thee;"* (Jeremiah 1:5a – KJV). God thought of you, and the moment He did, your spirit and soul began to exist in the spirit realm. In His immense love, He wrote a book about your life (see *Psalms 139:16, Hebrews 10:7*). Every day of your life was written according to His love for you. He planned the manifold life you are supposed to live, then He designed and fashioned you in your mother's womb. Why do you think it took nine months for you to be born? The hands of God were carefully forming you in the womb. He was taking time to be precise in adding each strand of hair, every fingernail, checking your blood vessels, cells, and nerves. He is incredibly involved in this process that He does in love. Having brought you out of the womb, He watches over you, knowing that being a citizen of earth, He will not interfere in your decisions. He still watches, waiting for that moment when you come to know that He loves you, He made you, and you turn to Him and call Him "Daddy." He waits, wanting to shower you with every good gift and blessing. He waits for you.

As a side note, some persons will ask, "What about babies who are born deformed or are stillborn?" This is not something that caught God off-guard; nothing does. He is great and mighty, superior in wisdom, and it is He who decides if and why He will allow the birth of these children. Remember, He is the Author and Finisher, the Potter; it is He who decides what kind of vessel is best for its purpose. I saw the Lord work in this manner once. This gentleman I know, a dear friend of mine, was on very, very bad terms with his brother-in-law. There was no one who could bring peace between the two. My mom and I, being family friends, decided that we would intercede on their behalf. Night after night, we prayed earnestly about the situation. Some weeks later, the gentleman, let's call him Mike, informed me that his lady was pregnant. The Lord at this point gave me a dream, showing me that something was wrong with this baby's blood, and the dream ended with the baby miscarrying. I did not share this dream. Instead, I began to pray for mercy, while still engaging the Lord with my mom.

Under normal circumstances, congratulations would be in order. However, Mike mentioned that he did not know how to tell his family without including his brother-in-law. I reasoned with him, asking him to bear in mind that the child will need love and support from the whole family. A few days passed, and he eventually swallowed his pride and made the call to his sister and her husband. Mike's brother-in-law was overjoyed to hear the news, and they talked out their differences and reconciled, vowing to put the past behind them and move forward as true brothers, and healing took place. Shortly after, about two weeks later, Mike told me that his lady had developed some complications and had a miscarriage. His brother-in-law was there to offer him support. I saw them soon after hanging out together at a jerk spot. I cried tears of joy to see them laughing and chatting. As I reflected on the scenario, I asked the Lord "Why?"

He revealed to me that He knew the depth of love these two men carried for children, so He provided one to break the chains of anger and bitterness, selfishness and pride, and bring forth divine healing. We cannot, at our level, understand why God does what He does, for it is done in superior wisdom. For now, this topic will be left, if the Holy Spirit leads, for another book.

We, on the other hand, because of sin, have been born into a fallen world and live carnal lives, rejecting His love day after day. How often have we broken His heart? Do not think for a moment that the great God of Heaven is void of emotion. He does feel; He feels everything to a higher and deeper degree than we can imagine. It is through Him that we get emotions. I began thinking about this shortly after I recommitted my life to Him, and began to wonder how sad He must be to see us living in reckless abandon when He is longing for that "Daddy" moment. When you read through the books of the Bible, you will see that He does all that a Father does to keep us on the right path in wisdom. He chose to give us free will, to decide whether to accept or reject Him, and He did that so when we choose to love and come to Him, we do it out of choice.

Do you know that the angels in Heaven marvel at us, yes, us (human beings)? They cannot understand how we love a God that we have not seen and have the audacity to believe that after going through this life, we are guaranteed an incorruptible inheritance in Him who died for us.

Unto whom it was revealed, that not unto themselves, but unto us they did minister the things, which are now reported to you by them that have preached the gospel unto you with the Holy Ghost sent down from Heaven; which things angels desire to look into. (1 Peter 1:12 - KJV).

In simple terms, the angels marvel at the gift of salvation. What a privilege and a wonder. So, you see, when you understand who you are and whose you are, it changes your perspective.

Interacting With the Holy Spirit

He revealeth the deep and the secret things, He knoweth what is in the darkness, and the light dwelleth with Him. (Daniel 2:22 - KJV).

Opening Of My Spiritual Eyes

There is a realm beyond our own that many people generally know exists but do not have access to. I always marvel at how easily people believe in the existence of ghosts, aliens, witches, vampires, and the spirit of dead people, but when it comes to the Holy Spirit, He is quickly dismissed, and a move by Him would be considered luck or coincidence. The Holy Spirit deserves to be honoured and acknowledged. He is the most important person on the earth right now.

Many have confirmed that He is a person by their own walk with Him. Jesus recognizes Him as such, and I too add my two cents; if you take the time to talk to Him, you will see that He is a unique person. We tend to forget that it is His likeness that forms our template; He is a Spirit, we are spirit, and it is our spirit that is the nucleus of our personality. Truly, we need to know that He is more powerful, accurate, accessible, loving, and interested in us than anything on the side of darkness. It is out of His everlasting love that the Holy Spirit humbled Himself, mirroring Jesus, and chose to come and dwell within our frail fallen human form.

But we have this treasure in earthen vessels, [to show] that the excellency of the power may be of God, and not of us. (2 Corinthians 4:7 – KJV – emphasis mine).

He has come as our Shepherd, Teacher, and Friend, and we need only receive Him.

I have not heard many accounts of *how* exactly someone's spiritual eyes are opened. I believe that it differs for each person, so I will share my experience. At about 2:30 one morning, I was in prayer with my eyes closed, and I was focused on the Lord Jesus. My brain began to register that there was some small movement going on before me. I was seeing a purple mist moving and curling like smoke while my eyes were still closed. I stopped praying and began to focus on this weird occurrence. The purple mist became stronger and more vivid in color, then I saw dull images being formed in the mist. I was not sure what was happening and, after a while, I opened my eyes. I thought it was a strange one-off experience.

The following four nights, as I prayed, it began to happen again. I would be quiet and observe. On the fifth night, when it began, I slowly began to see what looked like a landscape with a hill in the distance. I saw what looked like sticks on the hill and then, suddenly, I saw a skull and lightning, all with my eyes closed. Instinctively, I said, "Lord, what is this?"

"Golgotha," He responded. The hill was still distant, but as I looked again, I recognized that the sticks were indeed crosses. I opened my eyes and was still unsure how to label what had been happening. It dawned on me that I must be getting visions. I thanked the Lord, finished my prayer, and went to bed.

As time went on, I noticed that a pattern developed: purple mist led to different still pictures. As soon as the purple showed up, I began to focus and wait for what would be shown to me. Then in the last week of April 2019, I was preparing to leave for the airport to attend a conference in the United States. I was standing in my living room at about 10 am, and was asking the LORD to direct my path and cover me under His blood and calm my fears because I did not like flying; suddenly, I had a flash vision. This time my eyes were open. I saw my own feet covered in Jesus' blood all the way up above my ankles.

"What was that!" I exclaimed.

"Walk in the power of the blood."

I was puzzled and asked, "LORD, what does that mean?" I did not get a response. So off I went to the conference.

God of the Journey

When I returned home, I called my mother and shared the experience and asked what it meant. She said, "I'm not quite sure. The LORD may be showing you to walk by faith according to the Word of GOD." I did my own scriptural research but to no avail. I figured, *"I'll wait for the understanding."*

Every believer's walk is deeply personal, designed by GOD, and expecting anyone else to completely understand is sometimes very difficult. As I continued to seek Jesus daily, He began to give me scripture verses and passages and explain them to me. He began to share His thoughts and reveal my ministry to me. As I had these experiences, I shared with Marsha, and my mom, words of knowledge that I took dictation on through His Holy Spirit. I was in amazement that so much was happening so fast, but both women confirmed that what I was receiving from Jesus was all over the Bible. Remember, I was still in my baby stage and was not yet versed in scripture; however, I began to see tangibly how JESUS truly is the living WORD. I also began having very vivid dreams; some I understood, and others I did not. Then one night, as I was praying, I heard the Lord say, "Anoint yourself." I took up my bottle of olive oil and consecrated it. Next, the Holy Spirit said, "With this oil I seal you unto Myself" and pronounced a blessing over me. This is recorded in scripture:

In him you also, when you heard the word of truth, the gospel of your salvation, and believed in him, were sealed with the promised Holy Spirit, who is the guarantee of our inheritance until we acquire possession of it, to the praise of his glory. (Ephesians 1:13 – KJV).

Baptism of FIRE

I indeed baptize you with water unto repentance, but he that cometh after me is mightier than I, whose shoes I am not worthy to bear: He shall baptize you with the Holy Ghost, and with fire. (Matthew 3:11 - KJV).

One Sunday, while sitting in church, they announced that there would be a weekend conference that would allow us to have spiritual encounters with the LORD. Of special interest to me was the baptism of the Holy Spirit. I so badly wanted to speak in tongues. I had heard my mother pray in tongues all my life, and now when Marsha and I would pray, I would feel the power of God electrify the atmosphere. I had to have it. I went to my Father and asked if I could attend. I got no response, so I left it alone.

About two months passed and I visited church again. They were three weeks away from the event. I felt a stirring and asked my Father again if I could attend, and soon after I got His permission. In August 2019, I was there, excited to experience everything. There were various sessions that were powerful. I found that each time we assembled, as soon as worship began, I had to take off my sandals, not discerning what the Lord was preparing me for.

Dionne N. Moore

And He said, Draw not hither: put off thy shoes from thy feet, for the place whereon thou standest is holy ground. (Exodus 3:5 - KJV).

The night before the baptism service, I was so filled with fear and expectation, not knowing what to expect. Regardless, I had my own ideas of what I desired, and since the Word says "let your requests be made known unto GOD" (Philippians 4:6 - KJV), I began putting in my demands, "Lord, I want to be the first one to speak in tongues because, remember, pastor christen him pickney first, and, Lord, I don't want the regular type of tongues. Please make mine unique, like Chinese. YES, let me have Chinese tongues." Following that, I drifted off to sleep. I imagine that Jesus was probably sitting on my bed listening to me and smiling, shaking His head and saying, "This one."

We gathered early the next morning, and after a little housekeeping and a general explanation of what to expect, we went into worship. Not even five minutes in, I heard someone at the front of the room begin to speak in tongues. Then another, then another; slowly the room erupted in prayer, praise and tongues. I tried hard to focus on the Lord in that moment. Persons came by every now and again to pray over me, but nothing was happening. It felt like an hour or so had passed. I began to weep, "Lord, I need You to baptize me. They keep saying 'receive, receive,' but I don't know how. I've never done this before. I don't know the right words to say. You have to do this.

God of the Journey

You have to help me. I won't leave here the only person NOT baptized. Even if they lock me up in here, I'm not moving until You help me." I cried even more. Just then, I heard two people praying over me. They seemed to have thrown half a bottle of olive oil on my head. I paid no attention to them.

I was busy begging Jesus not to leave me out when slowly I began to feel a tingle in the bottom of my feet. I shifted my weight as I had been in a kneeling position all this time. I continued to pray and weep, well, I was bawling, to be honest. The feeling became more intense and began to travel up my ankles and up my calves. *"I seriously need to lose this weight; my feet are going numb in a weird way,"* I thought. No, I was not going to be distracted by this weird feeling and my weight issues, so I continued to pray. I was at my wit's end. By this time, the sensation was just below my knees. My feet felt as though they were literally on fire. I could feel sparks in my veins. That was when I heard the lady in the front row before me start speaking in tongues, my Chinese tongues! "Not fair, God," I said under my breath. What a sense of humor Jesus has.

The feeling settled just below my knees and began to intensify even more now. As much as I was feeling this fire in my feet, there wasn't any actual pain. I turned my attention back to God, "Jesus, please, I want to be baptized!" I was screaming this on the inside. I said, "What must I do? **"Do not doubt that you have received,"** the Holy

Spirit responded. I shifted my prayer from begging and began to thank GOD in faith. As I did this, I heard the Holy Spirit very loudly and strongly in my spirit utter the same sentence: **"Walk in the power of the blood."** Immediately, I felt this strong bubbling inside my tummy, and it was coming up fast. Before I could assess what to do, the bubble came up into my throat and I opened my mouth, and a long, loud, powerful scream came from my lips. Something washed over me. I was aware that my feet were now completely engulfed in flames of FIRE. I couldn't see the flames, but I felt them. I began crying again and kept repeating "Thank You, Jesus."

When I eventually regained my composure, I lifted my head and glanced around. The room was empty, except for about three people. Everyone else had gone to lunch. I stood up, but found it very difficult. My legs felt like lead, and the fire, while not as intense, was still very present. I sat for about fifteen minutes, soaking in all that had occurred. I got up and tried to walk to the lunch buffet. I was walking like a severely pregnant penguin. Someone asked if I was okay. I said sure. I never made it to the food. It took a full hour for me to be able to use my legs and by now most people had checked out and were leaving.

"I have designed a different life for you." These words drifted back to my mind. I was filled with awe and wonder. <u>Never</u> had I heard of anyone being baptized in this manner. Come to think of it, everyone else received tongues. I was the only one in that sitting who received this completely unique baptism. Even in the midst of trying to wrap my head around what this meant, and what to do with this unique experience, still I wondered "Why not tongues?"

"You must first learn to walk the walk before you talk the talk," the sweet Holy Spirit answered.

During this time, I was in the midst of completing my degree and, as is similar with most, my group members and I were in and out of sync. The closer we got to finalizing the thesis, the more intense the pressure became. I was at my wit's end and felt like throwing in the towel. I am sure many of you reading this book can relate. One day, while at work, I caved. No progress was being made, and time was against us. I didn't know what to do so I ran to my Father, He who had become my best friend. I threw myself on His knees and just let it all out. It was a real ugly cry, the "Daddy, I don't wanna!" cry. I poured my heart out and then said, "What do I do now?" Very calmly, in His still small voice, He responded, **"Philippians 4:6."**

Be anxious for nothing, but in everything by prayer and supplication, with thanksgiving, let your requests be made known unto GOD; (NKJV)

As soon as I read the first four words, a wall of release washed over me. I cried even more, only now because His endearing love was so tangible. What a glory to live in the love of Jesus. I gathered myself and thanked Him, knowing I was not alone and He would help me through this. I reported back to my duties.

Things improved for a few weeks, but then came time to do our defense and, at this point, things were so disorganized I went again into prayer, only this time I was telling Jesus that I was resolved that I would NOT be doing the defense. I said to Him "Lord JESUS, this whole process is ridiculous! I am NOT doing this defense. I need You to cancel it. Even if You don't cancel it, I'm not doing it!" Oh, I was resolute in my mind, and nothing and no one could sway me. Things continued to spiral out of control the closer we got.

D-DAY: our presentation was scheduled for late afternoon. We arrived at the institution at 9 am to practice, when suddenly my group member called me to say our lecturer had instructed us to present at 10 am. I said "That's madness! We are not ready!" They began to make calls back and forth for about half an hour with the lecturers, and chaos descended like a heavy storm with severe gale-force winds. I sat in my vehicle, very annoyed with everything and everyone, wondering why I came there in the first place. Then another phone call "Dionne, our presentation is cancelled for today." My eyes and mouth popped open.

"What did you just say?"

"CANCELLED. Our presentation is cancelled. They will let us know when we should present." The phone went dead. I went stone cold. That was the exact word I used to the Lord. The emotions I went through in those twenty seconds immediately following that are still indescribable. All I kept thinking was: "HE DID IT. HE CANCELLED IT!" Then I heard His voice, stern, in my spirit: ***"Is there anything impossible for ME? Do not rejoice because you must fulfill your responsibilities."***

I was completely humbled and felt convicted of my behaviour, "Yes, Father, I'm sorry," I responded. I quickly grasped at that moment that as my Father, He was willing to adjust the circumstances to allow me to breathe, but because I am HIS, it was not permissible to disregard my responsibilities. He is a GOD of order, and that is how He operates. It was continually being solidified through my experiences that most of what He says comes directly from His Word.

There have been many instances where the LORD has taught me how powerful He is, and how He truly loves His children. There was an instance when I tried to fast for the second time, and I asked Him not to let me smell any food because I was aware of my weakness. As I was sitting in the middle of a group of co-workers having their lunch, it dawned on me that I was not smelling anything. I was in awe. In spite of this, I wasn't as successful with the fast, and still struggle even now. As I mentioned, this relationship and all that is involved is a process.

The LORD Jesus has had to teach me many lessons on pride. You would be surprised how stealthily it creeps in. On one occasion, while I was at work, we had a little downtime, so I moved to the parking lot to rest. Shortly after, I heard very strongly in my spirit the word **"Immigration,"** and a close childhood girlfriend of mine, Seany, popped into my mind. I knew based on previous encounters that I was about to receive a word for her, and I immediately sat up and thought "Okay, something to put in our group."

"Okay, Lord, what shall I say to them?" I called all three of my girlfriend's names. He very sternly asked **"Who is going to get the glory?"** Oh, I curled right back up in my shell and apologized. I pulled out my pen and paper and waited for Him to speak. I delivered His message to my girlfriend and didn't give it another thought. She eventually messaged me, blown away to have received the same message twice in a short timeframe. To GOD be the glory. We must take ourselves out of the way and allow the LORD to use us. We are here to serve, and God rewards us in His way for our faithfulness.

There have been many teaching moments like this in different areas of my life. The most notable was a fast He instructed me to do. I was informed when to fast, what hours to pray, when to break the fast, what to eat, and why I was fasting. Around day four, upon breaking the fast, I had my veggies as was permitted, and then I decided to top it off with a peanut butter sandwich. This was within the hours I was allowed to eat. As I took the first bite, the Holy Spirit said **"I am watching you."** I rebutted, "Lord, I'm allowed to eat now." I put the bread to my lips a second time and I heard quite clearly and sternly **"This night you shall surely die."** FEAR GRIPPED ME and I flung the bread on the plate and ran to my room and shut the door, burst into tears, and begged for forgiveness. Whether He meant physically or spiritually, I did not know, nor did I want to find out. Our Father does not tolerate insolence. As any father does, He will watch to see just how far we will go, but there comes a time when He must chastise.

For whom the Lord loveth he chasteneth, and scourgeth every son whom he receiveth. If ye endure chastening, God dealeth with you as sons; for what son is he that the father chaseneth not? (Hebrews 12:6-7 - KJV).

Now I know you may be thinking, "Wow, that's so harsh and seemingly over the top," but, you see, it was measurable to the fast that He commissioned me to do; the purpose of the fast was very important and required very strict consecration. These experiences and many others have reinforced how intimately the Holy Spirit is involved in my life, and I am sure it is not nearly as involved as He would like to be.

Your relationship with Him need not be static, boring, or empty. He is not way off in space. He is constantly within you, quiet sometimes, but fully aware of what you are going through and what you are doing. Talk to Him plainly in a respectful manner; He is waiting.

The LORD is faithful, and He is also righteous. He is interested in every area of our lives. He truly wants to share in our joys and concerns or celebrations and disappointments. Believe me when I tell you that He is even interested in the clothes you want to wear and what facial products we use in our skincare. He also expects His children to operate in a spirit of excellence.

Many times, we live our lives in a mediocre fashion, but that is not our birthright in Christ. We ought always to remember that He is not just our Father, but our righteous Judge, our Commander-in-Chief, and we must obey His Word.

Relationship And Religion

In my first year with Christ, it was He who began to show me the difference between relationship and religion. Many persons are defensive about religion, and I can understand why. We have been cultured this way all our lives. We were taught to go to church and serve the LORD, end of story, but if we allow the Holy Spirit to lead us, we will not find ourselves on the side of error.

One night, very early after my recommitment, I had a dream. I dreamt that I was at the gate of Heaven and I was allowed to enter. As I did, the angel looked at me and said, *"The Lord requires you to go this way,"* and he pointed to my right. I turned and walked in the direction he instructed. I entered a hallway. It was made of concrete; it was very cold and drab. I kept going down this hallway and I noticed that the concrete walls had within it what looked like picture frames with faces, but they were not defined. It was a long hallway and, having walked a good distance in, I stopped and asked, "Lord, where is this?" I heard Him say, *"This is my church, which has gone cold and lifeless."* When I woke up, I did not know what to make of the dream except that I thought it was sad.

At the time I was attending a well-known church in Kingston, and was enjoying being saved. I would meet with my close girlfriend, Lanz, and we would go to church together. I was learning both from the church and from the Holy Spirit. One Sunday morning, as I was preparing to head out, I heard the Holy Spirit say, **"I have something to show you."** As we arrived, we were ushered into the tent on the outside. We began worshipping and went into prayer. As we stood there, the scripture reading was placed on the screen. I remember it was a passage from the book of Peter. I looked up and began to read, and I felt something like a rush of water being poured into me and, simultaneously, the whole sermon to be preached. I knew it was being downloaded into my spirit. It was an intense few seconds, and when it passed, I burst into tears. The Holy Spirit said, **"Now, pay attention to what I will show you."** Lanz turned and looked at me like I was weird. Her facial expression said, *"Geez, it was just a reading from the Word."* The service continued with the welcome and announcements. As I listened, I went into an open vision:

I was in Jerusalem observing Jesus from a distance, standing on a step about two up from the ground level, speaking to a multitude of people who were seated on the ground as well as the steps below Him. I saw clearly that all who were around Him were seated in the dust, engulfed in what He was saying. Then the vision ended. **"It doesn't take all this,"** the Holy Spirit said. I was deeply humbled at that moment, and I understood His lesson. The focus of church needs to go back to one simple thing: the message of CHRIST. It is this message that leads to true salvation: Christ Himself is the foundation of eternal life.

There is a distinction between 'the church' and 'THE CHURCH.' One represents the people who cry "Lord, Lord," and are workers of iniquity, as shown in Matthew 7:23:

And then will I profess unto them, I never knew you; depart from me, ye that work iniquity. (KJV).

In this statement, Jesus taught that many who called upon His name would have considered themselves 'safe,' but that word <u>knew</u> is incredibly significant. Jesus is teaching us that intimacy is also a qualifier for the Kingdom of GOD. The other CHURCH is the *true* bride of Christ, the one without wrinkles or spots. Many people are attending church but are not **BEING** the church. There is a commitment required of us to take up our cross daily and follow Christ:

Then said Jesus unto his disciples, If any man will come after me, let him deny himself, and take up his cross, and follow me. (Matthew 16:24 – KJV).

The doctrine being preached these days has a sprinkling of Jesus in it, but we are so far removed from the complete Word of God. Specific verses are "preached" from specific books in the Bible. Now we have a feel-good gospel, not the good news gospel, not the gospel that convicts men of sin and requires a persecuted, consecrated life, not the gospel that seats us in heavenly places in Christ Jesus for us to have dominion on earth, to take back what the enemy stole from us, not the gospel that calls us to be holy, and obedient to the King of kings, not the gospel that requires us to serve others in love and not think of self. This is the gospel the Holy Spirit was referring to: focus on JESUS, the Son of God, who died in our place and deserves all glory and praise.

We live in an age where we see the Word of God manifesting before us: actions that are evil are considered good, and what is good is considered evil, and the church has gone silent, no longer preaching what Jesus taught: that the wages of sin is death, but the gift of God is eternal life. We are not taught that we will be judged before a righteous Judge who sits on a throne with fire in His eyes. We are not taught that hell is real, and many will end up there for rejecting the love and gift of God. We are no longer taught to deny our own desires to build a spiritual life of power hinged on a relationship with a Saviour who is willing and able to teach us how to live victoriously and how to focus on the service of winning souls for the Kingdom of God. Instead, we are taught a "name it and claim it," watered-down prosperity gospel by preachers who seek to build wealth from their members. Friends, the Lord has not called us to a life of poverty, nor has He called us to a life of religion. He says:

God of the Journey

...seek ye first the kingdom of God, and His righteousness; and all these things shall be added unto you. (Matthew 6:33 KJV).

As the prototype of a good Father, He is looking to give us good gifts and rewards, both spiritual and physical, for living according to what He says.

The heart of God is broken, for His children have rejected Him. The world has been rocked to sleep in the arms of religion. If we would choose to have a relationship with the God of Heaven, and surrender to His will, the fire of God would ignite the church, and God's glory would fill the earth. His Word is true. We profess to be children of the King but deny His power. I encourage you today, if you hear God's voice, do not harden your heart. All He wants is to have a relationship with you.

Behold, I stand at the door and knock. If any man hears my voice, and open the door, I will come in to him, and will sup with him, and he with Me. (Revelation 3:20 - KJV).

SECTION 2:

THE BATTLE SERIES

For the weapons of our warfare are not carnal, but mighty through God to the pulling down of strong holds. (2 Corinthians 10:4 – KJV).

When you become a child of God, you are enlisted into a spiritual army and, often, the battle is fierce. This battle, Apostle Paul tells us, is not with flesh and blood. We fight spiritual battles daily that present themselves as "my world is over now" challenges (because we can be melodramatic at times, lol). The key is knowing how to fight. As my walk with Jesus began to move forward, He decided to equip me with a set of tools that every believer needs to have. The next few pages will walk you through His Word exactly how He taught me, verbatim, and we will see that these tools are the most basic but also the most lethal in your arsenal as a child of God.

The First Tool

We begin as He did in Matthew 9:20-22, with the woman with the issue of blood:

And, behold, a woman, which was diseased with an issue of blood twelve years, came behind him, and touched the hem of his garment: For she said within herself, If I may but touch his garment, I shall be whole. But Jesus turned him about, and when he saw her, he said, Daughter, be of good comfort; thy faith hath made thee whole. And the woman was made whole from that hour.

The lady with the issue of blood had uncommon faith. She did not even require Jesus' attention; she only needed to come in contact with something of who He is. In other words, her belief in His power to heal and transform her situation was all she needed. *"For she said within herself."* No one knew her thoughts; no one knew her intention; no one knew her desire. The woman reached out in faith and touched His garment. When we look at verse 22, we see a process that takes place, and so many people miss it.

<u>Jesus turned towards her:</u> her faith got His attention. He felt her faith.

God of the Journey

<u>When He saw her:</u> now she knew that He saw her, acknowledged her presence and her need.

<u>He said:</u> Jesus now spoke words of life into her situation. This is the process, and processes take time: (Faith + Time = Answers).

- We extend our faith to Him.
- He feels our faith.
- He lets us know He sees us.
- He speaks to us.

"Daughter, be of good cheer, your faith has made you whole." Restoration took place in that moment. Her faith took her into the very presence of the Healer and restored what she had lost. Hallelujah!

The Holy Spirt took me further to the next story recorded in Matthew 9:23-25:

And when Jesus came into the ruler's house, and saw the minstrels and the people making a noise, He said unto them, Give place: for the maid is not dead, but sleepeth. And they laughed him to scorn. But when the people were put forth, he went in, and took her by the hand, and the maid arose. (KJV).

The ruler's daughter had died, and an atmosphere was set for grief, confusion, mockery, and unbelief. There are times when the situations we are faced with are overwhelming to us, but it is at this moment that we must go in search of the one who calms the winds and waves. This is what our faith does: it invites Jesus into our fears, pain, doubt, confusion, sorrow and, by extension, the mockery and noise of those around us who are spectators of our faith. In the parable, it says the people were put out. He went in and took her by the hand and the maid arose. Understand that there are times when you must put out or turn away from people or situations in your life that foster chaos and focus on the Master. It was when all the noisemakers were gone that faith had a place to flourish. Miracles do not take place in an atmosphere of unbelief; they happen in that place of intimacy when your unwavering faith connects to the power of the living God. What a mighty God we serve!

The final story used in this lesson follows in Matthew 9:27-29:

And when Jesus departed thence, two blind men followed him, crying, and saying, Thou son of David, have mercy on us. And when he was come into the house, the blind men came to him: and Jesus saith unto them, Believe ye that I am able to do this? They said unto him, Yea, Lord. Then touched he their eyes, saying, According to your faith be it unto you. (KJV).

We notice from the first line that the men following Jesus were blind. They followed Him directly through hearing His voice. They cried out continually for mercy. They were so relentless that they followed Jesus into the house. The Holy Spirit impressed upon me how desperate these two men were to follow Him in faith, not knowing where they were going, hungering for His Word, His healing, His deliverance, His love. Jesus asked them a key question: "Believe Ye?" Even though they were following Him, they were still required to declare their faith in Him. The Word says, *"That if thou shalt confess with thy mouth the Lord Jesus, and shalt believe in thy heart that God hath raised Him from the dead, thou shalt be saved."* (Romans 10:9 – KJV). They answered "Yes, Lord." Jesus says: "According to your faith, be it unto you."

At this exact moment, I heard a viking battle horn in my spirit (the Holy Spirit uses props too!), and the Holy Spirit said: **"Unwavering faith is the first tool for the battle."**

I was immediately taken into an open vision, and I saw the Lord standing before me holding a bow and arrow, pointing it straight at me. I instinctively knew that the enemy was also behind me, using me as a shield. I saw the Lord pull back and release the arrow and it hit and killed the enemy. The Lord showed me how faith is used in battle: Our faith is the arrow God uses on our behalf. He knows how to use them, and He never misses! This is why we must partner with Him, know, and believe His Word, just like the woman with the issue of blood, the ruler, and the two blind men. We must participate in the process, extend our faith to our God and allow Him the time to fight the battles with and for us.

The Second Tool

The lessons that I was taught in this series were done on four consecutive mornings. I would like to pause here a moment and state that shortly after attending the church I mentioned in Kingston, the Holy Spirit stated very clearly that I should not return to church, and He would teach me what I needed to know. Now, this confused me as I was brought up in church, and I am not against attending church. There is a need to fellowship with believers to build foundational principles. Make sure you attend a Bible-based church that teaches all of the Word, and those who lead are sincere about your growth.

I began to search the Word about not attending church and soon came across the passage where Apostle Paul stated that after his conversion, he was not taught of man but by revelation through Christ Jesus (see Galatians 1:11-20). I was now settled in my heart that I was not going out in error, and true to His Word, the Holy Spirit held many classes with me in the wee hours of the morning. Friends, there is nothing He cannot do. The more we desire Him, the more He will reveal Himself to us.

On the second morning, promptly at 1:30 am, I presented myself to Him, my Teacher. He took me to John 12:1-8:

Then Jesus six days before the passover came to Bethany, where Lazarus was, which had been dead, whom he raised from the dead. There they made him a supper; and Martha served: but Lazarus was one of them that sat at the table with him. Then took Mary a pound of ointment of spikenard, very costly, and anointed the feet of Jesus, and wiped his feet with her hair: and the house was filled with the odour of the ointment. Then saith one of his disciples, Judas Iscariot, Simon's son, which should betray him, why was not this ointment sold for three hundred pence, and given to the poor? This he said, not that he cared for the poor; but because he was a thief, and had the bag, and bare what was put therein. Then said Jesus, Let her alone: against the day of my burying hath she kept this. For the poor always ye have with you; but me ye have not always. (KJV).

There is a sweetness in humility that love brings out. It was customary in those days to prepare a feast for your guests. Martha was busy waiting hand and foot, preparing and serving; however, Mary's focus was different. It was her joy to sit at the feet of her Master. She loved Him so much that she went and got her most expensive oil and poured it on Jesus's feet. This was her way of showing Him how much He meant to her. This is how we are called to worship. It was a sacrifice from her heart to worship Jesus in this manner. She was scolded by her sister and Judas Iscariot; they thought her silly, lazy, and irresponsible to sit idle and waste the oil.

There are people who will want to distract you and show you other ways to serve. There are those who wish to dissuade you from true worship and desire you to lose out on the presence of God. It is for us to understand the importance of who we are serving and what pleases Him. Jesus said in verse 7, *"Let her alone, against the day of my burying hath she kept this."* Jesus saw the sincerity in her worship and defended her, which allowed her to stay in a position of worship. Recognize that there will always be persons who do not come around you to get to know Jesus for themselves. They prefer to watch and criticize; they spectate like viperous snakes because of your devotion, because of your worship.

Keep in mind too that Mary existed in a space now defined by a miracle. This was evidenced by living in the same home with Lazarus. It was her pure, consistent worship that kept her in that space. Even with unbelief and criticism surrounding her, she did not lose focus on Jesus, her source. She insisted on staying and poured out her best form of worship to Him. Jesus comes to her defense and will defend us too.

Do not be discouraged. Be like Mary; worship in Spirit and in truth. Do as the song says: *"Forget about yourself"*— Mary was oblivious to what those around her said or thought she was doing—*"Concentrate on Him"*—our only true offering to God is worship—*"and worship Him"*—the Most High, Saviour and King.

Dionne N. Moore

"True worship is the second tool for the battle." —Holy Spirit

The Third Tool

On the third morning of class, the Holy Spirit decided to change things up a bit and began to speak directly to my spirit: **"For a time is coming when the son of man shall be cast into the sea. They shall neither hear nor see the goodness of God. Taste and see now that the Lord is good. Open your hearts and receive the love of God. Be ye transformed, not given over to the things of this world, but seek the kingdom of God, the sure way of Salvation. Remember thy neighbor, make peace with them, sin not, judge not, but press towards the mark, the high calling of Him who lives and reigns on high, for the love of God abounds. Though the foundation be torn away, yet will My Word stand."**

He then directed me to 1 Peter 2:1-12:

Wherefore laying aside all malice, and all guile, and hypocrisies, and envies, and all evil speakings, as newborn babes, desire the sincere milk of the word, that ye may grow thereby: If so be ye have tasted that the Lord is gracious. To whom coming, as unto a living stone, disallowed indeed of men, but chosen of God, and precious, ye also, as lively stones, are built up a spiritual house, an holy priesthood, to offer up spiritual sacrifices, acceptable to God by Jesus Christ. Wherefore also it is contained in the scripture, Behold, I lay in

Dionne N. Moore

Sion a chief corner stone, elect, precious: and he that believeth on him shall not be confounded. Unto you therefore which believe he is precious: but unto them which be disobedient, the stone which the builders disallowed, the same is made the head of the corner, and a stone of stumbling, and a rock of offence, even to them which stumble at the word, being disobedient: whereunto also they were appointed. But ye are a chosen generation, a royal priesthood, an holy nation, a peculiar people; that ye should shew forth the praises of him who hath called you out of darkness into his marvellous light; Which in time past were not a people, but are now the people of God: which had not obtained mercy, but now have obtained mercy. Dearly beloved, I beseech you as strangers and pilgrims, abstain from fleshly lusts, which war against the soul; having your conversation honest among the Gentiles: that, whereas they speak against you as evildoers, they may by your good works, which they shall behold, glorify God in the day of visitation. (KJV).

We are called to truly be set apart, to display/represent Jesus in every area of our lives. We stand as witnesses to this generation to be holy, regardless. It is our holy lifestyle that will be the light in the darkness to lead people to Christ. We must stand holy, so the accuser has no ammunition, nothing to use against us. If God calls us His people, how then can we disgrace Him with unholy living? The Israelites disgraced God when they erected idols in the wilderness. Will we do the same? Our wilderness is packaged in rejection, depression, lack of recognition from our peers, deceit, idle conversations, and unbelief. In all this, what will God's people look like? Do we represent our King well?

We cannot compromise in being obedient to God's Word, no matter how different we seem to family, friends, and coworkers. There must be a distinctness about you in the same way Peter was identified as one of Jesus' followers. 1 Peter 2:7-8 states that Jesus was the stone the builders threw away, which became a stumbling block and a rock of offence. Jesus did not conform or compromise to what the religious leaders of the day taught. He came with truth. He came with righteousness. His ways were an offence. Let your life also be an offence to cause people to see a commitment to righteous living, a standard of morals and principles that are contrary to common norms and traditions. Especially in this current century, the church should stick out like a sore thumb, the one swimming against the current in step with the Holy Spirit. Until we begin to embrace holy living, we will continue to be beaten and whipped by the enemy, and we will be unable to stand and represent our King.

"Righteousness is required for the battle." —Holy Spirit

The Fourth Tool

The final lesson in this series is from Acts 1:4-8, a familiar passage to all:

And, being assembled together with them, commanded them that they should not depart from Jerusalem, but wait for the promise of the Father, which, saith he, ye have heard of me. For John truly baptized with water; but ye shall be baptized with the Holy Ghost not many days hence. When they therefore were come together, they asked of him, saying, Lord, wilt thou at this time restore again the kingdom to Israel? And he said unto them, It is not for you to know the times or the seasons, which the Father hath put in his own power. But ye shall receive power, after that the Holy Ghost is come upon you: and ye shall be witnesses unto me both in Jerusalem, and in all Judaea, and in Samaria, and unto the uttermost part of the earth. (KJV).

Jesus instructs His disciples to stay in Jerusalem, to basically remain in a state of worship, obedience, patience, with a posture of expectancy, until the gift, the Holy Spirit, comes. His baptism is the gift of power. The fire is a promise, a right of being a child of God, and should be a natural part of our lives. It is a gift that takes faith to receive. God's fire is self-sustaining and renewing. The Holy

God of the Journey

Spirit already dwells within you; the baptism of fire provides the outside proof.

"The baptism of fire is another tool for battle. It gives immediate access to the throne." —Holy Spirit

Prayer as a Weapon

Many people know that there is good and evil, darkness and light, but many choose to live in denial that this evil is around and in them. We all consider ourselves good. We look at situations that unfold around us as luck, destiny, fate or, as we say in Jamaica, "boy, mi just salt." Persons have had encounters with demons; however, they are not acknowledged as that. Instead, it is termed the para-normal: something weird, seeing ghosts, dead relatives, strange dreams where different animals are attacking you, etc. If you have experienced any of these, you have had interactions with demons with a curly ribbon name around it. There is no need to get flustered and worried.

There are many believers who truly follow Christ and get squeamish at the thought of demons and cannot wrap their minds around it. That is okay, but it doesn't mean you are off the hook. It means you are standing in a place of loss and defeat.

As my walk began and progressed, I began to have strange dreams of big black dogs attacking me, tidal waves coming to knock down the building I was in, hyenas walking in and out of my living room, strange people trying to have sex with me; just all sorts. There were other times when I would walk into a shop, and someone would turn around and start quarreling with me about rubbish. I had to learn how to handle these situations. I knew and understood that these were spiritual attacks, so let us turn our attention to Ephesians 6:10-18. Most people read verses 12-17 and stop there; however, we miss what is available to us:

Finally, my brethren, be strong in the Lord, and in the power of his might. Put on the whole armour of God, that ye may be able to stand against the wiles of the devil. For we wrestle not against flesh and blood, but against principalities, against powers, against the rulers of the darkness of this world, against spiritual wickedness in high places. Wherefore take unto you the whole armour of God, that ye may be able to withstand in the evil day, and having done all, to stand. Stand therefore, having your loins girt about with truth, and having on the breastplate of righteousness; And your feet shod with the preparation of the gospel of peace; above all, taking the shield of faith, wherewith ye shall be able to quench all the fiery darts of the wicked. And take the helmet of salvation, and the sword of the Spirit, which is the word of God: Praying always with all prayer and supplication in the Spirit, and watching thereunto with all perseverance and supplication for all saints; (KJV).

I found out very quickly after recommitting my life to Christ that I was not only a new citizen of heaven but I was drafted into the army too. All of us are, to varying degrees. When we chose to turn away from sin, we become an 'enemy of the state,' and now all the tanks, guns, and grenades are being made ready to attack us. We are told this in 2 Corinthians 10, two blocks up the road from Ephesians, that the weapons of our warfare are not carnal. Knowing that, we now have to face these battles, which we may think are extremely hard, but the Lord is really using them for your growth and development. He allowed Apostle Paul to share with us the armor we have—and we have weapons too.

I won't get into the armour now, but be sure to read the passage and put it on daily. I want to take your attention to verses 10 and 18.

Permit me to squeeze these two verses together: *"Finally, my brethren, be strong in the Lord, and in the power of his might. Praying always with all prayer and supplication in the Spirit, and watching thereunto with all perseverance and supplication for all saints." (KJV).* Do you remember that other verse that says, "the prayer of a righteous man availeth much?" (KJV). Well, these two go hand in hand.

Prayer is a weapon. The Bible says we must take the sword of the Spirit. We know this is the Word of God. Prayer now becomes the way you use the sword. If you have ever watched one of those old Chinese movies where the actors have long samurai swords doing all kinds of dangerous moves, that is prayer! That is how it works. When we become skilled in prayer, the battles become easier. The devil doesn't know any fancy moves, so he is counting on you not to know any either.

One night I dreamt that I was standing by my baby's crib, and 'someone' pushed me over the crib and was trying to stab me. I began blocking the baby with one hand and fighting with the other. I was shouting "the blood of Jesus!" It ended very quickly, and I woke up panting. I felt defeated. I was miserable. I threw my hands up and said "Lord, when am I gonna make some kind of impact on the enemy?" Then the Lord replayed the dream before me, and I saw that as I was shouting 'the blood of Jesus," I had a dagger, and I was ramming it in the neck of the 'person,' and that was why it fled. I was so thankful, but it now opened my curiosity to understand exactly how powerful prayer can be.

Prayer is a mighty tool in battle that cuts bars asunder. It is the weapon the Holy Spirit uses in diverse ways to take down the enemy. Prayer can be used to wield the fire of the Holy Spirit and utterly destroy the camp of the enemy. Believe me, I have seen it with my own eyes. It can cut down the spirits of sickness, depression, suicide, and lust like branches on a half-dead tree. Prayer can build your faith and lower the blood of Jesus as a protective canopy over you and your family. Prayer is the most versatile weapon that the Father has given us access to. I don't know about you, but I am determined to wield my prayers like a samurai master.

Dionne N. Moore

When Apostle Paul said "Pray without ceasing" (I Thessalonians 5:17 - KJV), it is because there is always someone somewhere who needs our help. There is always a need for protection. Prayer does this. When you need wisdom from the Lord on how or what to pray, read Romans 8:26-27. There is no need to fear. The Holy Spirit lives inside us. Jesus intercedes for us, and the Father is protecting us.

CONCLUSION

This life we are called to live is never an easy one. It was not easy for Jesus either. In my own walk, I have fallen down many times, but my heart desires to be in that place where the presence of God becomes my own oxygen, so I get up, ask for mercy and forgiveness, and keep going forward. Having these interactions with Christ have had, and continue to have, a significant impact on me, and it continues to build my faith.

Faith is the substance, the core diamond of this relationship process. It is the foundation for you to begin to build your relationship as well, for without faith, it is impossible to please Him (see Hebrews 11:6). It is through your faith that you prove to God that you trust Him, His Word, and His timing for your life. This is what pleases Him.

Today, I encourage you, wherever you are on your journey with the Lord; at the very beginning or a few years in, if your relationship lacks intimacy and fire, begin to talk to Him, tell Him you desire to know Him, and know His love for you. It is my guarantee that the Holy Spirit will search your heart and see the sincerity you carry. As He reveals

Himself to you, your life with Him will begin to take on substance and stature.

There is so much to be said about the unfailing, incomprehensible love of God. David wrote, *"What is man, that thou art mindful of him? and the son of man, that thou visitest him? For thou hast made him a little lower than the angels, and hast crowned him with glory and honour. Thou madest him to have dominion over the works of thy hands; thou hast put all things under his feet."* (Psalm 8:4-6- KJV). No better question could have been asked.

The Creator has given all to His creation. What joy to be loved like this, and to be able to reciprocate this love. Align with Him, and study His Word. It will guide you. Pray often. Talk to your Father; He is waiting on you.

PSALM OF PRAISE

Psalm 146
Praise ye the Lord. Praise the Lord, O my soul.

While I live will I praise the Lord: I will sing praises unto my God while I have any being.

Put not your trust in princes, nor in the son of man, in whom there is no help.

His breath goeth forth, he returneth to his earth; in that very day his thoughts perish.

Happy is he that hath the God of Jacob for his help, whose hope is in the Lord his God:

Which made heaven, and earth, the sea, and all that therein is: which keepeth truth for ever:

Which executeth judgment for the oppressed: which giveth food to the hungry. The Lord looseth the prisoners:

The Lord openeth the eyes of the blind: the Lord raiseth them that are bowed down: the Lord loveth the righteous:

The Lord preserveth the strangers; he relieveth the fatherless and widow: but the way of the wicked he turneth upside down.

The Lord shall reign for ever, even thy God, O Zion, unto all generations. Praise ye the Lord. (KJV).

PRAYERS

Prayer to Receive Salvation

There has never been a time in history when anything has been more important than prayer. It would not please my Father if I closed this book without prayer—an opportunity for us to go before Him together.

If you have chosen to surrender your life to Christ and are not sure what the next move is, do what the Bible says, *"Confess with your mouth."* I choose now to stand with you and hold your hand as you purpose in your heart to totally surrender your life to our Christ. Please pray this prayer: **"Father in Heaven, I bow in this moment to honour You. Thank You for Your Son, Jesus Christ, who came to earth in the form of man to pay the price for my sin with His own pure blood. Jesus, I need Your forgiveness for my sins, and I humbly ask right now that You cleanse my heart and life by the power of Your blood. I turn away from my life of sinning and now choose to follow You in all Your ways. I receive and thank You for Your gift of Salvation, in Jesus' name. Amen."**

Congratulations!
You are now a new citizen of the Kingdom of Heaven.

Prayer to Recommit to Christ

There is much that we go through in life that causes us to become stagnant in our walk with God. Today, I dare you to trust Jesus again. I dare you to expect a new, fresh, love-filled relationship with the one you call Saviour. Choose to recommit to your first love and remind Him of His promise in 2 Timothy 1:12 "…for I know whom I have believed, and am persuaded that he is able to keep that which I have committed unto him against that day." (KJV).

As you choose to return to the arms of your Father, I choose to stand with you as you pray this prayer: **"My Father and King, I bow before Your throne, confessing that I have been wayward and unfaithful in my relationship with You. I have come to myself and found that I can do nothing without Your love, Your leading, Your presence in my life. Lord Jesus, please forgive me for all my sins; wash them clean with Your blood. Through Your grace and mercy, I recommit my life entirely to You, choosing Your will above my own. I ask now, Lord Jesus, that You begin to reveal Yourself to me again through Your Holy Spirit, and teach me the fullness of Your Word. Thank You for Your faithfulness to me. Thank You for restoring my life. I pray this, in Jesus' name. Amen."**

Welcome home!

Prayer For My Readers

It has been profoundly humbling to share this portion of my journey with you. I am filled with joy because I know the Holy Spirit will do a great work in your life. I pray with all sincerity that this book given by the Holy Spirit through me has blessed you and cracked open a desire to seek to be authentic with the God we serve, and with this, I pray: **"My God and King, Holy One, I bow in gratitude to You today for Your love towards us. I exalt You above all things and seek always to remain at Your feet. Jesus, thank You for every person who has read this book. Thank You for what You plan to do in their lives and for the faithfulness that is now birthed in their spirits. My Lord, I pray that You cover each reader with Your precious blood, that You arm them with the truth of who You are and whose they are, for in this confidence they shall stand against the adversary. Holy Spirit, I pray that this work You have begun will be a stepping stone that You have prepared for their journey with You. I pray that You continue to guide them on the path where their destinies will be accomplished according to Your Word. Bless them as they begin or continue this authentic journey with You, in Jesus' Name. Amen."**

May His love shine on and in you.

ABOUT THE AUTHOR

Dionne Moore began her walk by being called by God. Being bored by her childhood experience with religion, upon recommitment, she asked the Lord for a radical relationship. The Lord, in His mercy, granted this request. Now she lives in constant awe of her Saviour and is encouraging new and older Christians to connect with God in an authentic way that breaks the mold and hold of the republic of religion. As blood-washed believers, regardless of our stage in life, we can learn to walk in the freshness of the Holy Spirit. She now uses her life to lift the name of Jesus as a banner, pointing people to Him, showing that what God desires to have with every believer is not only possible, it is amazing. Fellowship with the uncreated God of the universe is readily available to anyone who wants to truly know and live with Christ.

www.ingramcontent.com/pod-product-compliance
Lightning Source LLC
Chambersburg PA
CBHW071315110426
42743CB00042B/2548